FUN FACT FILE:
FIERCE FISH!

20 FUN FACTS ABOUT MORAY EELS

By Heather Moore Niver

Gareth Stevens
Publishing

Please visit our website, www.garethstevens.com. For a free color catalog of all our high-quality books, call toll free 1-800-542-2595 or fax 1-877-542-2596.

Library of Congress Cataloging-in-Publication Data

Niver, Heather Moore.
20 fun facts about moray eels / Heather Moore Niver.
    p. cm. — (Fun fact file: fierce fish!)
Includes index.
ISBN 978-1-4339-6984-3 (pbk.)
ISBN 978-1-4339-6985-0 (6-pack)
ISBN 978-1-4339-6983-6 (library binding)
1. Morays—Juvenile literature. I. Title. II. Title: Twenty fun facts about moray eels.
QL638.M875N58 2012
597'.43—dc23

                          2011049951

First Edition

Published in 2013 by
Gareth Stevens Publishing
111 East 14th Street, Suite 349
New York, NY 10003

Copyright © 2013 Gareth Stevens Publishing

Designer: Ben Gardner
Editor: Greg Roza

Photo credits: Cover, pp. 1, 10 Brian Lasenby/Shutterstock.com; pp. 5, 6 PBorowka/Shutterstock.com; p. 7 © iStockphoto.com/Marcus Lindström; p. 8 tagstiles.com–Sven Gruene/Shutterstock.com; p. 9 Stubblefield Photography/Shutterstock.com; pp. 11, 15, 26 Dray van Beeck/Shutterstock.com; p. 12 FAUP/Shutterstock.com; p. 13 Borut Furlan/WaterFrame/Getty Images; p. 14 tubuceo/Shutterstock.com; p. 16 Rich Carey/Shutterstock.com; pp. 17, 24 James A Dawson/Shutterstock.com; p. 18 Dan Exton/Shutterstock.com; p. 19 Song Heming/Shutterstock.com; p. 20 Tobias Bernhard/Oxford Scientific/Getty Images; p. 21 vilainecrevette/Shutterstock.com; p. 22 cbpix/Shutterstock.com; p. 23 Ernie Hounshell/Shutterstock.com; p. 25 Stephen Frink/Photographer's Choice/Getty Images; p. 27 © iStockphoto.com/Sharon Metson; p. 29 Levent Konuk/Shutterstock.com.

Printed in the United States of America

CPSIA compliance information: Batch #CS12GS: For further information contact Gareth Stevens, New York, New York at 1-800-542-2595.

Contents

Words in the glossary appear in **bold** type the first time they are used in the text.

Mysterious Morays

Moray eels might seem a bit confusing. They're long and skinny like snakes, but they swim in the water like fish. Some people even think they look like aliens. Moray eels may seem like they're from out of this world, but they're definitely fish.

Close to 800 different species, or kinds, of eels swim in Earth's waters all over the world. More than 100 of them are called moray eels. They belong to the scientific group Muraenidae (myuh-REE-nuh-dye). Morays can be found in all **tropical** waters.

This giant moray eel comes out of its hiding spot to smile for the camera!

At Home with Morays

Moray eels like shallow water with good hiding spots.

Like most fish, moray eels are cold-blooded animals. They prefer to make their home in the warmer waters of tropical and **subtropical** seas. Moray eels swim in shallow water where there are **coral reefs** and rocks to hide in during the day.

Fish Without Scales

Moray eels are fish without scales.

The moray eel has a long, muscular body. Most fish have scales, but not the moray eel. Its smooth, thick skin is covered by **mucus**, which helps it speed through the water. Mucus also protects the moray's skin from rough, rocky surfaces.

The honeycomb moray eel, shown here, gets its name from the pattern on its skin.

Fin Facts

FACT 3

The moray eel has one long fin that runs from its head to its tail.

Moray eels are easy to spot among other fish. They have one long dorsal, or back, fin that runs the whole length of their body. Unlike other eels, morays don't have pectoral, or chest, fins.

A moray eel's dorsal fin helps it move through the water.

dorsal fin

Moray eels are tipsy swimmers.

Moray eels don't have pectoral or **pelvic fins**, which makes them look more like snakes than fish. Without these fins, moray eels tend to tip to the side. They're often found floating around on their sides or even upside down!

Green morays are actually blue, but the yellowish mucus on their skin makes them look green.

FACT 5

Moray eels are so colorful they've earned the nickname "painted eel."

A moray eel's skin is often brightly colored or patterned. They can be striped, spotted, or speckled. Morays can be lots of different colors, too. They may be brown, green, white, yellow, black, or even blue. Sometimes they're called painted eels because they're so colorful.

Take a Deep Breath

The moray eel's method of breathing often earns it a bad name.

Fish breathe by moving water over their **gills**. Moray eels have very small gills, so they open and close their mouth constantly to keep water flowing over them. Many people mistake this way of breathing for anger.

This is a yellowmouth moray eel.

11

Eel Eyes

FACT 7

Moray eels can smell much better than they can see.

Moray eels have small heads, with eyes toward the front. They have tiny eyes and poor eyesight. Luckily, they have a great sense of smell, so they can easily sniff out their next meal.

People trying to touch or feed moray eels have lost fingers because the fish usually can't see the difference between the food and the person!

Long, Lean Eel

Morays can grow to be up to 13 feet (4 m) long.

The fact that there are lots of different kinds of moray eels means that they come in all kinds of sizes. The green moray can grow to more than 8 feet (2.4 m) long. The slender giant moray can grow to a length of 13 feet (4 m).

Most moray eels aren't longer than 5 feet (1.5 m).

green moray eel

THE MIGHTY MORAY!

common name	where they are found	longest
slender giant moray	Indo-Pacific	13.1 feet (4 m)
giant moray	Indo-Pacific	9.8 feet (3 m)
laced moray	Indo-Pacific	9.8 feet (3 m)
green moray	western Atlantic	8.2 feet (2.5 m)
viper moray	Indo-Pacific	8.2 feet (2.5 m)
yellow-edged moray	Indo-Pacific	7.9 feet (2.4 m)
spotted moray	western Atlantic	6.6 feet (2 m)

common name	where they are found	longest
Griffin's moray	southwest Pacific	5.9 feet (1.8 m)
starry moray	Indo-Pacific	5.9 feet (1.8 m)
speckled moray	eastern Pacific	5.6 feet (1.7 m)
chain moray	western Atlantic	5.4 feet (1.65 m)
California moray	eastern Pacific	5 feet (1.52 m)
stout moray	eastern Atlantic	4.9 feet (1.5 m)
Mediterranean moray	eastern Atlantic and Mediterranean	4.9 feet (1.5 m)

giant moray eel

Munching Morays

Peppered moray eels almost swim out of the water to catch a meal.

Morays are **nocturnal**, so night is their favorite time to hunt. They find most of their food very close to their homes. However, peppered morays have been known to come into such shallow water for a tasty treat that they risk getting stuck on land!

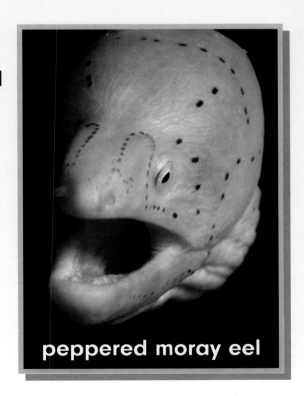

peppered moray eel

Weak or injured fish are the moray's favorite snack to sniff out.

Moray eels eat fish, cephalopods (squids, cuttlefishes, and octopuses), **mollusks**, and **crustaceans**. They use their great sense of smell to snatch snacks. Weak or injured fish are the easiest to find in the dark.

FACT 11

Moray eels don't dine out very often.

Moray eels spend much of their time in narrow holes between rocks or in coral reefs. When a moray eel is hungry, it doesn't travel far. It waits for **prey** to swim within reach, darts out, grabs it, and enjoys some fresh meat.

Terrible Teeth!

A moray eel's teeth slant backward to stop prey from escaping.

Moray eels have a wide, strong mouth that's good for biting down on prey. These **predators** have mouths filled with strong, pointy teeth. A moray's teeth slant backward to keep prey from slipping out once the moray has chomped down.

Moray eels have a second set of toothy jaws in their throat.

Moray eels are among about 30,000 fish species that have two sets of jaws. The second jaws are called pharyngeal (fuh-RIHN-jee-uhl) because they are located in the pharynx, which is between the mouth and the tube to the stomach.

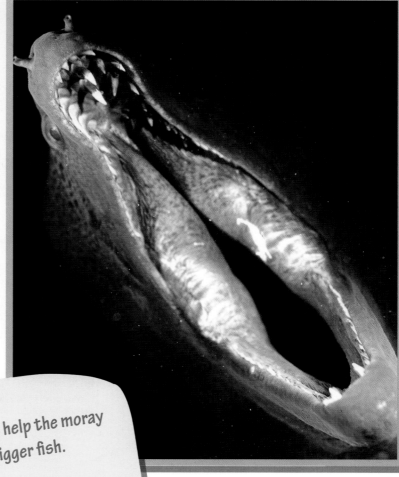

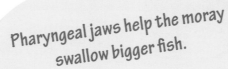

Pharyngeal jaws help the moray swallow bigger fish.

The moray eel's pharyngeal jaws reach up out of their throat to grab prey.

Other fish species use their extra jaws to squeeze and swallow their prey. Only the moray eel uses them to yank its meal into its throat. The jaws move forward, clamp down on prey, and then move back into the pharynx.

Eel Eggs

FACT 15

Baby moray eels take about 2 years to grow up.

Baby morays hatch from eggs. The babies, called **larvae**, are small and clear. They float in the water for 8 months. During that time, they grow into small morays called elvers. Then they swim down and hide in a reef to continue growing.

Many moray larvae are eaten by other sea creatures before they grow to be elvers.

Moray eels live between 6 and 36 years.

FACT 16

Some morays begin life as a male but later become female.

Scientists have learned that just because a moray eel is born as a boy or a girl doesn't mean it will stay that way. Some are born male, but change to become female. Other morays are both male and female at the same time!

Fishy Friends

Moray eels have their own personal cleaning service.

Small shrimp and cleaner wrasse are good friends with moray eels. They're kind of like living toothbrushes! The shrimp and wrasse feed on **parasites** and bits of food in the mouths of moray eels.

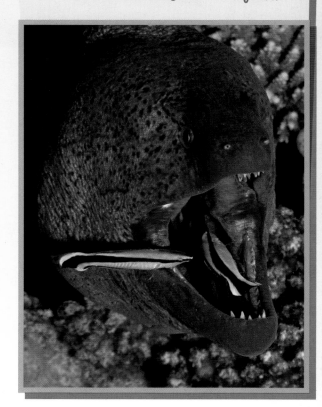

Two cleaner wrasse find lunch in the mouth of a giant moray eel.

Eek! An Eel!

Some moray eels have poisonous bites.

Moray eels don't usually attack humans. They only strike if they feel they're in danger. **Toxins** in the moray's mouth can be poisonous, but its bites aren't deadly. Getting chomped on by all those teeth sure hurts, though!

Moray eels' toxins are called "ichthyotoxins," which means "fish poisons."

Ancient Romans enjoyed eating Mediterranean moray eel. They even raised them in special ponds.

FACT 19

King Henry I of England may have died from dining on moray eel.

The moray eel's only real threats are other morays, large fish like groupers and barracudas, and people. Some people fish for morays, but they're not good to eat because they contain toxins. Some say that King Henry I died after eating one.

Moray eels can be good pets, but watch your fingers!

Some people keep moray eels as pets, but they can be dangerous. Most kinds of moray eels don't make good pets. However, some smaller morays—including zebra, snowflake, and starry morays—enjoy tank life.

Even small moray eels can be very forceful. Only people who know a lot about raising fish should keep them as pets.

Excellent Eels

Moray eels swim in shallow waters in and around coral reefs. These long, strong fish can even chow down on fish larger than them. Thanks to the work of two impressive pairs of jaws, the moray gets plenty to eat.

So if you ever get the chance to swim or dive near a reef, be sure to keep a lookout for these fantastic fish. Just remember to keep your hands away from their mouths, or you might get bitten. Moray eels are a sight to see!

Glossary

coral reef: a strip of coral near the surface of the water

crustacean: an animal with a hard shell, jointed limbs, feelers, and no backbone

gill: the body part that ocean animals such as fish use to breathe in water

larvae: the early form of an animal, usually right at birth or hatching. "Larvae" is plural. "Larva" is singular.

mollusk: a water animal that doesn't have a spine but has a shell

mucus: a slimy coating made by animals

nocturnal: active at night

parasite: an animal that lives with, in, or on another animal

pelvic fin: a fin that is similar to the back leg of a four-legged animal

predator: an animal that hunts other animals for food

prey: an animal hunted by other animals for food

subtropical: having to do with areas near the tropics

toxin: a poison produced by an animal

tropical: having to do with warm areas near the equator

For More Information

Books

Goldish, Meish. *Moray Eel: Dangerous Teeth.* New York, NY: Bearport Publishing, 2010.

Gross, Miriam J. *The Moray Eel.* New York, NY: PowerKids Press, 2006.

Rothaus, Don P. *Moray Eels.* Chanhassen, MN: Child's World, 2007.

Websites

Green Moray Eel
www.aqua.org/animals_greenmorayeel.html
Learn more about the green moray eel.

Moray Eel
a-z-animals.com/animals/moray-eel/
Check out photos, facts, and more about the mighty moray eel.

Nature's Perfect Predators: Moray Eels
videos.howstuffworks.com/animal-planet/
36033-natures-perfect-predators-moray-eel-video.htm
Watch a video about moray eels and see them in action.

Index